Top 5 Mistakes That Immigration Attorney Firms Make with Online Marketing and How to Correct Them

The top 5 factors you need to fix that are keeping you hidden from the people who are looking for you

Table of Contents

Introduction 5
Mistake 1 7
    Neglecting Optimization of Google Business Profile 7
        Importance of Accurate Information 7
        Managing Reviews Effectively 8
        Consistent Content Posting 9
        Engaging with an experts 9
    Conclusion 10
Mistake 2 11
    Underestimating the Impact of SEO Optimization 11
        Importance of Local SEO for Immigration Attorneys 11
        Managing Reviews and Reputation 12
        Consistent Content Creation and Distribution 12
    Conclusion 13
Mistake 3 15
    Overlooking the Potential of PPC Advertising and Google AdWords. 15
        The Significance of PPC Advertising 15
        The Importance of Professional Management 16
        The Synergy Between PPC and SEO 16
        The Power of Repeat Exposure and Branding 17
    Conclusion: Embracing the Power of PPC Advertising 18
Mistake 4 19
    A Pretty Website vs Prioritizing User Experience 19
        The Psychology of User Experience 19

The Importance of Mobile Optimization 20
Driving User Action Through Effective Formatting 20
Leveraging Landing Pages for Targeted Lead Generation 21
Conclusion: Elevating Website User Experience for Enhanced Lead Generation 22

Mistake 5 23
Not Unlocking the Power of Email Marketing for your Firm 23
The Power of Email Marketing 23
Nurturing Leads Through Email Sequences 24
Automating Email Marketing Efforts 24
Maximizing Engagement and Conversion 25
The Enduring Effectiveness of Email Marketing 25
Conclusion: Harnessing the Potential of Email Marketing 26
Unlock Your Firm's Potential Today! 27
Table of Resources 29

Introduction

Welcome to "Top 5 Mistakes That Immigration Attorney Firms Make with Online Marketing and How to Correct Them." In today's digital age, establishing a strong online presence is essential for the success of any business, including immigration attorney firms. However, navigating the complexities of online marketing can be daunting, especially with the ever-evolving landscape of search engines, social media platforms, and digital advertising channels.

In this ebook, we'll delve into the five most common mistakes that immigration attorney firms make with their online marketing efforts and provide actionable strategies to help you overcome these challenges and achieve greater success in your practice. From neglecting optimization of Google Business Profiles to underestimating the impact of SEO optimization, each chapter will explore a key area of concern and offer practical solutions to help you maximize your firm's online visibility, attract more qualified leads, and ultimately, grow your practice.

As you embark on this journey to optimize your online marketing strategies, I would like to dedicate this ebook to Tara Hartman. Tara, your unwavering support and belief in me have been a constant source of strength and inspiration, especially during the toughest of times. Your resilience, compassion, and unwavering faith have shaped me into the person I am today, and I am eternally grateful for your presence in my life. This ebook is a testament to your unwavering support and belief in me, and I dedicate it to you with heartfelt gratitude and appreciation.

Let's dive in and unlock the full potential of your immigration attorney firm's online marketing efforts together.

Mistake 1

Neglecting Optimization of Google Business Profile

In today's digital landscape, an optimized Google Business Profile has become a cornerstone of success for businesses across various industries, including immigration law firms. Neglecting to optimize your Google Business Profile can significantly impact your firm's visibility, reputation, and ultimately, its ability to attract and retain clients. In this chapter, we'll explore why optimizing your Google Business Profile is crucially important for immigration attorneys and provide actionable strategies to maximize its effectiveness.

Importance of Accurate Information

Your Google Business Profile serves as a virtual storefront for your immigration law firm, providing essential information to potential clients who are searching for legal services online. It is crucial to ensure that this information is accurate, up-to-date, and comprehensive. This includes your firm's name, address, phone number, website URL, business hours, and a brief description of your services.

Accurate information not only helps potential clients find and contact your firm with ease but also establishes trust and credibility. Inaccurate or outdated information can lead to confusion, frustration, and even loss of potential clients. Therefore, regularly review and update your Google Business Profile to maintain its accuracy and relevance.

Managing Reviews Effectively

Client reviews play a significant role in shaping your firm's online reputation and influencing potential clients' decision-making process. Positive reviews can enhance your credibility and attract new clients, while negative reviews can deter potential clients and damage your firm's reputation.

It is crucial to actively manage your firm's reviews on Google Business Profile, Yelp, and other review platforms. Respond promptly and professionally to all reviews, whether positive or negative, to demonstrate your commitment to client satisfaction and address any concerns or feedback.

Implementing a review filtering system can help maintain a positive online reputation. By filtering out negative reviews (those below a certain star rating) from public view and promoting positive reviews, you can ensure that your firm's online presence reflects its strengths and successes accurately.

Consistent Content Posting

Regularly posting content on your Google Business Profile and other review platforms is essential for maintaining a strong and active online presence. Posting content such as updates, articles, case studies, client testimonials, and educational resources not only keeps your profile fresh and engaging but also helps boost its visibility in search results.

Consistent content posting demonstrates your firm's expertise, credibility, and commitment to serving your clients' needs. It also provides valuable information to potential clients, helping them make informed decisions about hiring legal representation for their immigration matters

Engaging with an experts

Hiring a specialized agency to manage your Google Business Profile can significantly enhance your online visibility and increase your firm's chances of appearing in both organic search results and the coveted Google Maps 3-pack. With expert optimization strategies, your profile can achieve dual placement on Google search pages and maps, maximizing exposure to potential clients. The Google Maps 3-pack showcases the top three most relevant or recommended businesses for a given search query, making it a prime location for attracting leads. Achieving placement in this pack requires careful management of reviews, reputation, and information accuracy—areas where a specialized agency excels. Additionally, a reputable agency can implement advanced digital marketing tactics such as press releases, external blogs, and citation building, which further boost the authority of your Google Business Profile and website. By targeting broader geographical areas through strategic press releases and content distribution, your firm can expand its reach and outshine competitors in neighboring cities and counties, solidifying its position as a trusted leader in immigration law services.

Conclusion

Optimizing your Google Business Profile is not just about filling out a form; it's about strategically leveraging this powerful tool to enhance your firm's online visibility, reputation, and client acquisition efforts. By providing accurate information, managing reviews effectively, and posting consistent content, you can maximize the impact of your Google Business Profile and position your immigration law firm for success in the digital age. By leveraging the expertise of a specialized agency to handle this process automatically, you can unlock the full potential of your profile and elevate your firm's online presence. From securing dual placements on Google search pages and maps to strategically targeting broader geographical areas through advanced digital marketing tactics, such as press releases and content distribution, the opportunities for growth and visibility are vast. By investing in professional management of your Google Business Profile, you can position your immigration law firm for long-term success in the digital age.

Mistake 2

Underestimating the Impact of SEO Optimization

In the competitive landscape of immigration law, neglecting to optimize your firm's online presence for local search engine optimization (SEO) can be a costly mistake. Local SEO is the process of optimizing your digital presence to attract more business from relevant local searches on Google and other search engines. In this chapter, we'll delve deeper into the importance of local SEO optimization for immigration attorneys and explore the strategies to maximize your firm's visibility and reach within your target geographic area.

Importance of Local SEO for Immigration Attorneys

Local SEO is crucial for immigration attorneys as the majority of potential clients seeking legal assistance prefer to work with a local attorney who understands the intricacies of local immigration laws and regulations. By neglecting local SEO optimization, you risk missing out on valuable opportunities to connect with potential clients in your area and losing them to competitors who have a stronger online presence.

One of the key components of local SEO optimization is ensuring that your firm's information is accurately and consistently listed across online directories, review platforms, and social media channels. This includes your firm's name, address, phone number, website URL, and other relevant details. Inaccurate or inconsistent information can confuse potential clients and harm your firm's credibility and visibility in local search results.

Managing Reviews and Reputation

In addition to listing accuracy, managing online reviews and reputation is paramount for local SEO success. Positive reviews signal trustworthiness and credibility to potential clients, while negative reviews can deter them from contacting your firm. Implementing a review management system that filters and responds to reviews promptly can help maintain a positive online reputation and enhance your firm's visibility in local search results.

A specialized agency can assist immigration attorneys in implementing effective review management strategies, including filtering out negative reviews below a certain star rating and promoting positive reviews to improve your firm's online reputation and attract more clients.

Consistent Content Creation and Distribution

Consistent content creation and distribution are also critical components of local SEO optimization. By regularly posting informative and engaging content related to immigration law on your website and social media channels, you can establish your firm as a thought leader in your area and attract more qualified leads.

Furthermore, distributing content through external channels such as press releases, guest blog posts, and local directories can help boost your firm's visibility and authority in local search results. A specialized agency can assist in creating and distributing high-quality content that resonates with your target audience and drives more traffic to your website.

Conclusion

In conclusion, neglecting local SEO optimization can have significant repercussions for immigration attorneys, including reduced visibility, loss of potential clients, and decreased competitiveness in the market. By prioritizing local SEO optimization and implementing effective strategies, such as managing reviews and reputation, creating and distributing consistent content, and ensuring listing accuracy, immigration attorneys can enhance their online presence and attract more clients in their target geographic area.

However, it's essential to recognize that SEO is an extremely time-consuming process that requires ongoing effort and expertise in areas such as on-page optimization, link building, content creation, and keyword research. Hiring a specialized agency to handle your firm's SEO efforts can help you reap the benefits of increased visibility and traffic while allowing you to focus on what you do best—engaging with clients and providing expert legal representation.

SEO is like owning real estate in a busy street where your storefront is exposed constantly to potential clients who can buy goods from your storefront without having to pay a company to bring them in. This organic traffic is invaluable as it provides a steady stream of leads without the ongoing cost of PPC advertising. Investing in SEO is a long-term investment in your firm's success, positioning you as a trusted authority in immigration law and generating valuable leads and clients for years to come.

Mistake 3

Overlooking the Potential of PPC Advertising and Google AdWords

Pay-per-click (PPC) advertising, particularly through platforms like Google AdWords, is a game-changer for immigration attorneys seeking to expand their online presence and attract qualified leads. In this chapter, we'll delve into the intricacies of PPC advertising, with a special emphasis on Google AdWords, and explore how leveraging this powerful tool can accelerate your firm's growth and success.

The Significance of PPC Advertising

PPC advertising offers immigration attorneys a unique opportunity to showcase their services to potential clients at the exact moment when they're searching for legal assistance online. Through platforms like Google AdWords, attorneys can bid on keywords relevant to their practice areas and display targeted ads to users across various Google properties, including search results, maps, YouTube videos, Gmail, and partner websites.

The beauty of PPC advertising lies in its precision targeting capabilities. Unlike traditional advertising methods, PPC allows you to reach users who are actively seeking legal services related to immigration law, ensuring that your ads are seen by those with the highest likelihood of conversion. By harnessing the power of Google's vast network and sophisticated targeting options, immigration attorneys can effectively connect with potential clients and drive meaningful engagement with their firm.

The Importance of Professional Management

While PPC advertising offers immense potential for success, it's not without its challenges. Managing PPC campaigns effectively requires a deep understanding of the platform's intricacies, including keyword selection, bidding strategies, ad copy optimization, and performance tracking. Without the requisite expertise, immigration attorneys risk squandering their advertising budget on ineffective campaigns that yield minimal results.

Indeed, we've witnessed firsthand the pitfalls of DIY PPC management, with clients inadvertently spending thousands of dollars per day on clicks with little to show in terms of tangible outcomes. This underscores the critical importance of entrusting your PPC campaigns to experienced professionals who possess the knowledge, skills, and resources to deliver optimal results.

The Synergy Between PPC and SEO

While PPC advertising offers immediate visibility and results, it should ideally be complemented by a robust search engine optimization (SEO) strategy for long-term success. SEO, akin to buying real estate in the digital realm, requires time and patience to yield substantial returns. However, when paired with PPC, it can amplify your firm's online presence and maximize your visibility across search engine results pages (SERPs).

Unlike PPC, which delivers instantaneous results, SEO operates on a slower timeline, with the effects gradually building over time. By investing in both PPC and SEO simultaneously, immigration attorneys can strike a harmonious balance between short-term lead generation and long-term brand building. As SEO gains traction and begins to drive organic traffic to your website, the budget allocated to PPC can be adjusted accordingly, resulting in a more efficient and sustainable marketing strategy.

The Power of Repeat Exposure and Branding

One of the key benefits of combining PPC and SEO is the ability to achieve repeat exposure across multiple touchpoints within search results. By dominating the SERPs with multiple listings—such as paid ads, organic search results, and Google Maps placements—immigration attorneys can establish a formidable presence that outshines competitors and instills trust and confidence in potential clients.

Psychologically, repeat exposure plays a pivotal role in branding and consumer decision-making. According to marketing studies, individuals are more likely to engage with a business or brand after multiple exposures, with the magic number often cited as five or more. By strategically positioning your firm across various search results, you can increase the likelihood of engagement and conversion, ultimately driving growth and success for your immigration law practice.

Conclusion: Embracing the Power of PPC Advertising

In conclusion, PPC advertising, particularly through platforms like Google AdWords, offers immigration attorneys a potent tool for expanding their online reach and attracting qualified leads. By leveraging the precision targeting capabilities of PPC and pairing it with a comprehensive SEO strategy, attorneys can establish a dominant presence within search results and outshine competitors in the digital landscape.

However, it's essential to recognize that PPC advertising is not a set-it-and-forget-it endeavor. Professional management and ongoing optimization are crucial for maximizing the effectiveness of your campaigns and maximizing your return on investment. By partnering with a specialized agency that understands the nuances of PPC advertising, immigration attorneys can unlock the full potential of this powerful marketing channel and achieve sustained growth and success for their firms.

Mistake 4

A Pretty Website vs Prioritizing User Experience

Understanding the psychology of user experience is crucial for immigration attorneys seeking to maximize the effectiveness of their websites and drive meaningful action from potential clients. In this chapter, we'll delve into the intricacies of website user experience and explore how optimizing your site for usability, accessibility, and conversion can significantly impact lead generation and client acquisition.

The Psychology of User Experience

Human attention spans are notoriously short, particularly in today's fast-paced digital landscape. Users browsing the internet are bombarded with information and stimuli, making it imperative for websites to capture and retain their attention effectively. A website that is cluttered, slow to load, or difficult to navigate is likely to frustrate users and drive them away, regardless of how visually appealing it may be.

Conversely, a website that prioritizes user experience by presenting information clearly, concisely, and intuitively is more likely to engage and convert visitors into leads. This involves optimizing the layout, content, and functionality of your website to ensure a seamless and enjoyable browsing experience across devices, including mobile phones.

The Importance of Mobile Optimization

With an increasing number of users accessing the internet via mobile devices, mobile optimization has become paramount for website success. A mobile-friendly website not only improves user experience but also enhances search engine rankings, as Google prioritizes mobile-friendly sites in its search results.

Ensuring that your website is optimized for mobile devices involves adopting responsive design principles, optimizing page load times, and streamlining navigation for smaller screens. By catering to the needs and preferences of mobile users, immigration attorneys can effectively reach and engage a broader audience and drive more leads through their websites.

Driving User Action Through Effective Formatting

Optimizing website user experience goes beyond aesthetics—it's about driving specific user actions that align with your firm's goals. Whether it's prompting visitors to provide their contact information in exchange for valuable resources, such as immigration law tips or case assessments, or encouraging them to schedule a consultation, every element of your website should be designed to facilitate user action.

This often involves incorporating clear and compelling calls-to-action (CTAs) throughout your site, strategically placing them in prominent locations to capture visitors' attention and guide them towards conversion. Additionally, forms should be formatted in a way that simplifies the lead qualification process, making it easy for users to provide the necessary information and initiate contact with your firm.

Leveraging Landing Pages for Targeted Lead Generation

In addition to optimizing your main website, creating dedicated landing pages can further enhance your lead generation efforts. Landing pages are standalone web pages designed to promote specific services or offers and drive user action. By directing paid campaign traffic to targeted landing pages, immigration attorneys can increase the likelihood of conversion and maximize the return on their advertising investment.

Moreover, landing pages can be optimized for SEO to improve their visibility in search results, further extending your firm's reach and attracting more qualified leads. By strategically leveraging landing pages in conjunction with PPC advertising and SEO, immigration attorneys can establish a dominant online presence and outperform competitors in terms of visibility and lead generation.

Conclusion: Elevating Website User Experience for Enhanced Lead Generation

In conclusion, mastering website user experience is essential for immigration attorneys looking to drive action and generate leads effectively. By understanding the psychology of user behavior and optimizing their websites accordingly, attorneys can create a seamless and engaging browsing experience that encourages visitors to take the desired actions.

From mobile optimization and effective formatting to leveraging landing pages for targeted lead generation, every aspect of website user experience plays a critical role in driving conversion and attracting potential clients. By prioritizing user experience and continually refining and optimizing their websites, immigration attorneys can position themselves for sustained success in the digital age and maximize their impact in the competitive legal landscape.

Save your chat history, share chats, and personalize your experience.

Mistake 5

Not Unlocking the Power of Email Marketing for your Firm

Email marketing has emerged as a potent tool for immigration attorneys seeking to engage with potential clients, nurture leads, and drive meaningful action. In this chapter, we'll explore the transformative impact of email marketing and delve into strategies for leveraging this powerful channel to maximize lead generation and client acquisition.

The Power of Email Marketing

Email marketing offers immigration attorneys a direct and personalized way to connect with prospects and build lasting relationships. Unlike traditional forms of advertising, which cast a wide net and rely on mass dissemination, email marketing enables attorneys to target specific segments of their audience with tailored messages and offers.

One of the key advantages of email marketing is its effectiveness in driving traffic to your website, lead pages, and Google profile. By offering valuable resources, such as ebooks, guides, or newsletters, in exchange for visitors' email addresses, attorneys can capture valuable contact information and transform anonymous website visitors into qualified leads.

Nurturing Leads Through Email Sequences

Once you've obtained a prospect's email address, the real magic of email marketing begins. Email sequences, consisting of a series of informative and engaging emails sent over a period of time, allow attorneys to nurture leads and guide them through the decision-making process.

A well-crafted email sequence can provide valuable insights into recent changes in immigration law, specific situations that may apply to a certain state, or common challenges faced by immigrants. By delivering relevant and timely content to your audience, you can position yourself as a trusted advisor and authority in your field, earning their trust and building rapport over time.

Automating Email Marketing Efforts

While email marketing can be incredibly effective, it can also be time-consuming to manage manually. Fortunately, there are tools and platforms available that allow attorneys to automate their email marketing efforts, saving time and ensuring consistent communication with leads.

Automated email marketing platforms enable attorneys to set up predefined email sequences that are triggered based on user actions, such as signing up for a lead magnet or visiting specific pages on your website. This ensures that leads receive timely and relevant communications without requiring manual intervention.

Maximizing Engagement and Conversion

In addition to nurturing leads, email marketing can also be used to maximize engagement and conversion. Crafting compelling subject lines that entice recipients to open your emails is crucial for capturing their attention and driving action. Additionally, attorneys can leverage email marketing to offer special discounts or incentives to encourage recipients to schedule a consultation or take the next step in the client intake process.

The Enduring Effectiveness of Email Marketing

In an era dominated by social media and digital noise, email marketing remains one of the most effective tools for driving engagement and conversions. While it may not garner the same attention as flashy social media campaigns, statistics and studies consistently indicate that email marketing boasts higher open and click-through rates, making it a valuable asset for immigration attorneys seeking to grow their practices.

Conclusion: Harnessing the Potential of Email Marketing

In conclusion, email marketing represents a powerful opportunity for immigration attorneys to connect with prospects, nurture leads, and drive meaningful action. By leveraging email marketing to deliver valuable content, automate communication efforts, and maximize engagement and conversion, attorneys can position themselves for sustained success in the competitive legal landscape.

While email marketing may require initial investment in terms of time and resources, the long-term benefits far outweigh the costs. By prioritizing email marketing as a key component of their overall marketing strategy, immigration attorneys can establish themselves as trusted authorities in their field and attract a steady stream of qualified leads and clients to their practices.

Unlock Your Firm's Potential Today!

Congratulations on completing "The Top 5 Mistakes Immigration Attorney Firms Make with Online Marketing and How to Correct Them." You've taken a significant step towards optimizing your firm's digital presence and driving sustainable growth.

As a token of our appreciation for your commitment to improving your practice, we'd like to offer you a complimentary 15-minute discovery call. During this call, we'll conduct a thorough analysis of your current immigration law firm's visibility and provide you with a comprehensive marketing strategy and plan of action tailored to your specific needs and goals.

This invaluable report and consultation are entirely free of charge, with no obligation whatsoever. We believe in empowering immigration attorneys like you to make informed decisions about their marketing efforts and achieve consistent, predictable results.

At the conclusion of your discovery call, you'll have the option to implement the recommended strategy independently or enlist our expert team to handle it for you. With our proven track record and commitment to excellence, you can trust us to execute your marketing strategy with precision and efficiency, allowing you to focus on what you do best: serving your clients.

Don't let common marketing mistakes hold your firm back any longer. Schedule your complimentary discovery call today and unlock the full potential of your immigration law practice!

"Get a FREE Visibility Audit and Competition Analysis, along with your streamlined executable Marketing Strategy and Plan. Everything you need to know to claim top visibility in your city and increase your client intake consistently. Visit today!"

http://BoostLegalVisibility.com

We look forward to helping you achieve your goals and elevate your firm to new heights of success!

Best regards,

William Alexander | CEO/Founder

Business Marketing Solutions, Inc

Table of Resources

1. Manage Your Google Business Profile Link
https://www.google.com/business/

2. Moz: The Beginner's Guide to SEO Link
https://moz.com/beginners-guide-to-seo

3. Google Ads a Starter Guide Link
https://support.google.com/google-ads/answer/6146252

4. Unbounce: The Landing Page Course Link
https://unbounce.com/lead-generation/lead-generation-landing-pages-free-ecourse/

5. The Best Email Marketing Platforms
https://zapier.com/blog/free-email-marketing-software/

These resources offer valuable insights and guidance on managing your Google Business Profile, understanding SEO principles, leveraging PPC advertising with Google AdWords, creating effective lead pages, and choosing the right email marketing platform for your needs.

www.ingramcontent.com/pod-product-compliance
Lightning Source LLC
Chambersburg PA
CBHW050254230526
45470CB00005B/2268